## Dedication

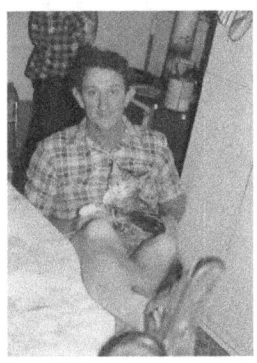

*This project has been called a crime of passion and is very much dedicated to my Father, Kevin Pitt. When I bought the WB back in 1988, a little known fact is that we went halves in the purchase. The ute found its way back to him for a year in the early 90's before returning to the farm in 1994 for its final stint and served him loyally until it was unable to be driven through mechanical failure.*
*Dad, wish you could have seen it restored to the full glory and even today, it is one thing that will always belong to the both us.*
*Miss you heaps.*

## Foreword

Where to start? "Ready for Action" the advert yelled. The Holden WB Series was the last of the Kingswood's as General Motors Holden marketed the new Commodore range. This model and series were the last to wear the Kingswood badge, a series that started in 1968 with the HK model though to 1984 with the end of production of the WB.

Every story and partnership has its beginnings and mine is with a 1981 build Holden WB series, which was an automobile range that was produced by General Motors Holden (GMH) in Australia from 1980 to 1984. My WB at Buhse's Garage in Laidley Queensland. The stories that I plan to share in this collection are my reflections of a vehicle that was part of my past life and remains a focus of it today. My WB was a glorious Holden White (or Palais White to be a little bit fancy).

The WB carried a face-lifted version of the previous model the Holden HZ series. Unlike the HZ and every other full-size Holden series before it, the Holden WB was

## Foreword

only offered in commercial vehicle body styles with no sedan or wagon passenger car variants.

There were the long-wheelbase models in the WB series, but they were marketed under the separate Statesman marque, absent of all Holden branding.

In the mid 1970's, Holden was faced with extremely difficult decisions about which direction to take, principally arising out of actions taken by oil producing countries overseas, which had restricted supplies to world markets and caused serious increases in fuel costs. Although the floated WA model (which was not produced) and WB projects at Holden were meant to have resulted in all-new full-size cars, the 1973 fuel crisis and cost-cutting meant the scope of changes became more limited each time.

Car buyers were, for the first time, faced with the need to consider fuel consumption and the vehicles currently under production in Australia were pretty uneconomical. Japanese vehicles had made considerable inroads on the Australian market due to their low price, comparatively high levels of standard equipment and fuel efficiency. Holden, Ford and Chrysler were all forced to re-think the types of vehicles they were going to replace their current models with.

There was a nervousness and understandable trepidation about the VB Commodore not only within some of the Holden's community as well as company headquarters. This turned out to be justified due to its smaller size than the rival Falcon and what the Commodore 4 cylinder could have been. As a back-up plan, Holden conjured up the WA Kingswood; a six-window design with a shovel nose front end to modernise the HZ. However, it went with the two-car strategy of VB Commodore and WB Statesman/Ute.

Eventually, the WB project was condensed into a major

## Foreword

upgrade of the luxury Statesman models and a facelift of the HZ-series commercial models with new headlights, taillights, grilles and the updated Holden "Blue" six-cylinder engine (4.2-litre V8 optional). The Kingswood was now available on utility only with the panel van joining the One Tonner, but the 5.0-litre V8 engine was no longer officially offered as an available performance option although some were built. There were no passenger car versions of the Kingswood, their place in the Holden range having been absorbed by the Commodore. Production of the entire WB-series finished in 1984 when Holden announced they were vacating local production of large luxury and commercial vehicles—due to economics—to concentrate on their medium car range, i.e. Camira and Commodore, and imported Isuzu commercial product.

What would have happened if Holden developed the WA instead of the Commodore, one could only surmise. The Commodore itself has certainly settled into the Australian physic as one of our iconic brands. Settle back with your favourite brew and enjoy a tale of a young man finding his way in the world and his beloved ute. The following stories are all true to the best of my recollection and memory.

# When the Phoenix Rises

# Mark Pitt

Love Books Publishing

Copyright © 2020 by Mark Pitt

All rights reserved.

No part of this book may be reproduced in any form or by any electronic or mechanical means, including information storage and retrieval systems, without written permission from the author, except as provided by United States of America copyright law. For permission requests, write to the publisher, at "Attention: Permissions Coordinator," at the address below..

Ebook ISBN 978-1-922369-14-7

Paperback ISBN 978-1-922369-15-4

*Love Books Publishing (Aus)*
*PO Box 373*
*Kingaroy QLD 4610*
*Australia*

## Contents

| | |
|---|---:|
| The story of the WB Ute in the Marketplace | 1 |
| Specifics of the WB | 4 |
| In The Beginning | 16 |
| Back to the Farm | 18 |
| Laid To Rest | 20 |
| The Plan is Enacted | 21 |
| Restoration of the WB | 23 |
| Finishing Touches | 40 |
| Restored and Returned | 41 |
| Acknowledgments | 45 |
| Notes | 47 |

## The story of the WB Ute in the Marketplace

According to Tim Nicholson who writes for RACV, the loss of Holden to the Australian populace would send "shockwaves through the automotive industry and spelled the end for one of Australia's most iconic brands. The 160-year-old Holden name, as much a part of our cultural fabric as meat pies, football and kangaroos, will cease to exist as GM is also closing its factory in Thailand, which produces Holden's Colorado."

At this time it means that the protection of the Holden vehicle is now of the utmost importance because, simply put, there will be no new cars rolling off the production line, and those remaining will potentially slip away into mythology.

For me, the cultural phenomenon known as Holden was embodied by Holden's own WB Utility.

Holden Australia produced the iconic WB Ute (Utility) between the years of 1980 and 1984, replacing the HZ series vehicle.

As with other full-size Holdens the WB was offered as a commercial vehicle only. That meant no sedan or passenger vehicles were available to the public. The long wheelbase of the WB was marketed under a Statesman badge, thus having none of the traditional Holden branding.

First released in April 1980, the range consisted of a panel van and a cab chassis utility. The Kingswood panel van, Sandman and the Sandman panel van did not carry over.

As a result, the only available vehicles were:
- Holden (utility and van)
- Holden Kingswood (utility)
- Holden One Tonner (cab chassis)

Featuring the black grate style grill and the rectangular headlights, the Kingswood stood out from the basic models.

In August 1980, the model was updated, granting it the same front as the traditional Kingswood.

When the series was discontinued in late 1984, there were supposedly plans to produce both a sedan and wagon of this model however the new Holden Commodore moved into the family market.

The discontinued WB and its Statesman variant had sales totalling 60 231, and while no replacement for the model was initially touted, the market hole would again be filled from 1990 with a VN Commodore based VG utility being released.

The end of the WB saw the conclusion of a 34-year run of light commercial vehicle offerings from Holden.

## Specifics of the WB

With sincere appreciation to Unique Cars & Parts for this information [1]
Years of Manufacture: 1980 - 1985
Number Built: 60,231

**Price at Introduction:**

Utility: $6971
Kingswood Utility: $7640
Kingswood Panel Van: $7167
One-Tonner: $6,940
Statesman DeVille: $14,790
Statesman Caprice: $19,769

**Models:**

Holden Utility
Holden Panel Van
Kingswood Utility
Kingswood Panel Van

One-Tonner
Statesman DeVille
Statesman Caprice
Statesman DeVille Series II
Statesman Caprice Series II
HDT Magnum

**Date(s) of Introduction:**

Panel Van, Utility, Kingswood Utility and One-Tonner: 20th April, 1980
Statesmans: 22nd June, 1980
Commercials (with revised grille): August, 1980
Statesman Series II: August, 1983

**To Identify:**

Similar body to HZ with seperate grille and headlights
Kingswood Utility with redesigned front nose section with grille and headlights
Early model WB's have circular headlights, grey grille with three holes and grey divider with Holden badge located above the grille
Kingswood and late model WB (from August 1980 onward) use rectangular headlights and a black grate style grille and the Holden badge now located in the centre of the grille
WB Statesman features slightly shorter but taller body over HZ, and incorporates a new "third" rear window
Statesman DeVille has thick bar grill with "DeVille" emblem located on lower left corner
Statesman Caprice has grille with thinner bars to

DeVille, making for a more elegant and refined appearance, and featuring integrated "Caprice" emblem
Brock Statesman Magnum features Momo aero-disc wheels, colour coded bumpers.
Series II Statesmans have special decals identifying them, and new badging

**Body:**
Unitary construction (Monocoque)

Full Chassis (Commercials)
Exterior Dimensions:
Total Length:
Utility: 4938mm
Panel Van: 4945mm
One-Tonner: 4897mm
Statesman: 5157mm

**Total Width:**

Utility, Panel Van and One-Tonner: 1877mm
Statesman: 1899mm
Total Height at kerb weight:
Utility: 1395mm
Panel Van: 1603mm
One-Tonner: 1420mm
Statesman DeVille: 1370mm
Statesman Caprice: 1390mm

**Wheelbase:**

All models: 2895mm

**Front Track:**

Commercials: 1520mm
Statesman Caprice: 1531mm
Statesman DeVille: 1523mm

**Rear Track:**

Commercials: 1530mm
Statesman Caprice: 1540mm
Statesman DeVille: 1536mm

**Kerb Weight:**

Utility: 1360kg
Kingswood Utility (6 Cylinder): 1370kg
Kingswood Utility (8 Cylinder): 1404kg
Panel Van (6 Cylinder): 1432kg
Panel Van (8 Cylinder): 1476kg
One-Tonner (6 Cylinder): 1292kg
One-Tonner (8 Cylinder): 1336kg
Statesman Caprice: 1719kg
Statesman DeVille: 1681kg

**Turning Circle:**
All Models: 12.3 metres

**Fuel Tank Capacity:**
Commercials: 70.4 litres
Statesmans: 91 litres (optional 126 litres)

**Instruments:**

Statesman:

Speedometer with integrated odometer and trip meter
Petrol gauge
Oil pressure gauge
Temperature gauge
Voltmeter
Digital Clock (Caprice)
Analogue Clock (DeVille)
Tachometer (Caprice)
Warning lamp cluster including warning lamps for brake system failure, hand brake, high beam, turning signal, taillamp failure, door adjar, low fuel, seat belt

3.3 202 Engine (Commercials):
Capacity: 201.25 cubic inches (3.298 litres)
Type: Conventional, watercooled four stroke, reciprocating piston type with 6 cylinders
Configuration: Front mounted, longitudinal, inline
Head: Pushrod and rocker actuated ohv with two valves per cylinder
Fuel System: GM Strasbourg Varajet twin barrel downdraft carburettor
Bore and Stroke: 92.1 x 82.5mm
Power:
Manual Transmission: 83kw at 4000rpm
Torque: 231Nm at 2400rpm
Compression Ratio: 8.8:1

253 4.2 Litre V8 Engine (Commercials):
Capacity: 252.8 cubic inches (4.142 litres)
Type: Conventional, watercooled four stroke, reciprocating piston type with 8 cylinders

Configuration: Front mounted, longitudinal, Vee configuration
Head: Pushrod and rocker actuated ohv with two valves per cylinder
Fuel System: Rochester Quadrajet four barrel downdraft carburettor
Bore and Stroke: 92.1 x 77.8mm
Power
Single exhaust : 100kw at 4200rpm
Dual Exhaust: 115kw at 4400rpm
Torque
Single exhaust : 269Nm at 2000rpm
Dual Exhaust: 289Nm at 3200rpm
Compression Ratio: 9:1

308 5.0 Litre V8 Engine (Statesman DeVille & Caprice):
Capacity: 307.8 cubic inches (5.044 litres)
Type: Conventional, watercooled four stroke, reciprocating piston type with 8 cylinders
Configuration: Front mounted, longitudinal, Vee configuration
Head: Pushrod and rocker actuated ohv with two valves per cylinder
Fuel System: Rochester Quadrajet 4BBL downdraft carburettor
Bore and Stroke: 101.6 x 77.8mm
Power: 126kw at 4400rpm
Torque: 361Nm at 2800rpm
Compression Ratio: 9.2:1

308 5.0 Litre V8 Engine (HDT Statesman Magnum):
Capacity: 307.8 cubic inches (5.044 litres)

Type: Conventional, watercooled four stroke, reciprocating piston type with 8 cylinders
Configuration: Front mounted, longitudinal, Vee configuration
Head: Pushrod and rocker actuated ohv with two valves per cylinder
Fuel System: Four Barrel downdraft carburettor
Bore and Stroke: 101.6 x 77.8mm
Power: 188.2kw at 5000rpm
Torque: 428.8Nm at 3500rpm
Compression Ratio: 9.2:1

**Ignition and Electrical:**

Commercials:
12 volt with 40 amp alternator (55 amp if air-conditioning fitted)
Pre-engaged drive starter motor
High energy breakerless ignition with 8mm silicone rubber insulated fibreglass core ignition leads

Statesmans:
12 volt with 55 amp alternator
62 amp battery
Pre-engaged drive starter motor
High energy breakerless ignition with 8mm silicone rubber insulated fibreglass core ignition leads

**Exhaust:**

Commericals:
6 Cylinder: manifold seperating first 3 from last 3 cylinders, entering into twin outlet flange with dual

exhaust pipes leading into a single pipe, muffler and tail pi4pe

8 Cylinder: Seperate front exhaust pipes from each side of the engine, with a cross-over into a single rear pipe to the muffler, and a single rear tail pipe

Statesman:
Seperate pipe and resonator assemblies from each side of the engine leading into dual mufflers. Each muffler in turn with intermediate pipe to single muffler at rear left hand side of car

HDT Statesman Magnum:
HDT exhaust manifod combined with high performance exhaust system

## Transmission Options:

3-speed (M15)
4-speed (M20, M21, M22)
Tri-matic (M40), Turbo 350 (M38)
Note: Turbo boxes were deleted around august 1982 and replaced with Tri-matics (308 only).

Utility and Panel Van - 3 speed Manual Transmission (3.3 six and 4.2 V8):
1st: 3.07:1
2nd: 1.68:1
3rd: 1.00:1
Reverse: 3.59:1

Utility and Panel Van - Optional 4 speed Manual Transmission (3.3 six and 4.2 V8):
1st: 3.05:1

2nd: 2.19:1
3rd: 1.51:1
4th: 1.00:1
Reverse: 3.05:1

Utility and Panel Van - Optional Tri-Matic Automatic Transmission:
1st: 2.31:1
2nd: 1.46:1
3rd: 1.00:1
Reverse: 1.85:1

Statesmans - Turbo-Hydramatic 400 Automatic:
1st: 2.48:1
2nd: 1.48:1
3rd: 1.00:1
Reverse: 2.08:1

**Clutch:**
GMH diaphragm single dry plate
Belleville diaphragm

**Rear Axle Ratio:**

Commercials (excluding One Tonner): 3.55:1
One-Tonner: 4.44:1 (optioanl 3.36:1)
Statesman: 3.08:1
Statesman towing/performance option: 3.36:1
Statesman Series II: 2.60:1

**Top Speed in Gears:**

Statesman DeVille (126kw version):
1st: 70 km/h

2nd: 140 km/h
3rd: 175 km/h
0-100 km/h: 9.7 seconds
Standing Quarter Mile (400 metres): 17.0 seconds

Kingswood 253 4.2 litre V8 Utility manual:
1st: 65 km/h
2nd: 90 km/h
3rd: 130 km/h
4th: 170 km/h
0-100 km/h: 12.2 seconds
Standing Quarter Mile (400 metres): 17.8 seconds

Statesman Caprice:
1st: 72 km/h
2nd: 122 km/h
3rd: 180 km/h
0-100 km/h: 11.8 seconds
Standing Quarter Mile (400 metres): 18 seconds

Statesman DeVille:
1st: 48 mph (78 km/h)
2nd: 82 mph (132 km/h)
3rd: 103 mph (165 km/h)
0-100 km/h: 10.9 seconds
Standing Quarter Mile (400 metres): 18.6 seconds

HDT Holden Statesman Magnum:
1st: 111 km/h
2nd: 175 km/h
3rd: 200 km/h
0-100 km/h: 9.43 seconds
Standing Quarter Mile (400 metres): 16.76 seconds

## Suspension:

Commercials:
Front: Independent, coil springs
Rear: Independent, coil springs

Statesman:
Front: Independent with short and long arms, coil springs, decoupled stabiliser bar
Rear: Four-link system with coil springs, decoupled stabiliser bar

## Steering:

Commercials:
Standard: Front-mounted recirculating ball type. Standard ratio 25:1
Optional power assisted: Integral variable ratio gear with rotary type control valve and hydraulic pump. Ratio varies from 18:1 to 11.7:1

Statesman:
Integral variable power steering, ratio 18.1:1

## Brakes:

Commercials:
Front: Power assisted discs standard
Rear: Drums, duo-servo

Statesman:
Front: Power assisted 276mm ventilated discs
Rear: Power assisted 293mm solid discs

**Wheels:**

Commercials:
Steel 6.00JJ x 14

Statesman:
DeVille: Steel with full wheel cover, 6.00JJ x 14 standard
Caprice: Styled cast alloy, 7.00JJ x 15 standard
HDT Magnum: Momo alloy, 7.00JJ x 15 standard

**Tyres:**

Commercials:
Utility and Panel Van: FR78S14 x 4 steel belted radials
One-Tonner: 195R14LT x 8 steel belted radials
Statesman:
DeVille: FR 78 H15
Caprice: ER 60 H15
HDT Magnum: Pirelli P6 235/30 VR 15

## In The Beginning

I bought the WB in early 1988, from Buhse's in Laidley. Buhse's became Llewellyn Motors and closed its Laidley presence in April 2019. (Incidentally, they sold the ute to its original owner in 1982, from what I have discovered.) It was traded back to Buhse's when I became the second owner.

It originally was registered as 434ACZ when I purchased it, and later was registered as 103AZF after being de-registered for 12 months.

*At the Farm circa 1988*

As a family we all went into Laidley to pick up the ute. We had seen it previously and Dad had, in his normal subtle style, negotiated the price. "You must be cracked man if you think we will pay that" if memory serves me right was the opening salvo. Dad was a ferocious negotiator and he use to school me on the fact that business was business. Mum generally went down the street to do any shopping that she had in mind while the business was done. Fortunately, we had previous experience with the WB model as Dad had been selling agricultural equipment for a company in Gatton – Agricultural Requirements.

*The WB by the barn on the farm circa 1988*

He had been given a work utility which was the same model. Very quickly he came to realise that you could easily disconnect the odometer cable, so it didn't calculate mileage. That meant that Mum, Dad and I could drive from our family farm in Blenheim to Bribie Island and back without running up the mileage. Dad would fuel the ute on Friday night, and we would leave for Bribie at about 3 am on Saturday morning – getting over there to cook a bbq breakfast on the beach. A day's fishing and looking around, occasionally (but rarely staying over) and heading back that night. He would reconnect the speedometer cable on Sunday after he had refilled the vehicle and head off to work selling agricultural equipment and no harm was done to any soul.

We bought the ute home and the bonnet went up. The anti-pollution gear on the 3.3. litre Holden blue engine came off and the rest, as they say, is history.

During the years of 1988 to 1994 I drove the ute anywhere and everywhere in Queensland. Anywhere I had to go, it went.

In 1989 I moved to Brisbane. During this time I worked as a Youth Officer and drove it to Far North and Western Queensland and all points in between while carrying out my role.

## Back to the Farm

In 1994 I married, and within twelve months the family was expanding and we needed a family car - everyone telling me you couldn't put a baby seat in the back tray (yes, that's a joke). The Ute unfortunately couldn't accomodate a baby seat inside either, so the ute started the next stage of its life as a working farm vehicle on my parent's farm in Blenheim.

During this time it did some truly amazing things, including carting a *bona fide* tonne of apples from Stanthorpe to Blenheim for my parent's market stall. (Sadly, no photos seem to exist of these endeavours!)

The ute also drove miles in visits, including up to Julia Creek before we moved to Thargomindah. My parents also loved to visit Charleville and the image shows it in 2001 parked alongside a caravan.

My parents drove it weekly and became a fixture at the various markets. They had an

 awesome set up, with the trailer hauling the hay and tents, while whips, books and preserves along with craft work travelled in the bed of the truck, which they sold direct from the ute-bed.

Eventually age and disrepair brought it to its thought to be final resting place, parked up on the hill at the farm.

*The market set up - she did an amazing job*

## Laid To Rest

My wife was always clear, when there was time and space it would eventually return.

It took around 15 years to get to the point of making a plan and organising to have it collected, during which the vehicle continued to deteriorate on the hill.

*The Ute on the side of the hill at the farm.*

## The Plan is Enacted

In August 2013 I travelled down to Gatton from Gayndah with Norm (the mechanic) driving the flatbed truck that would collect the Ute.

*Dad (Kevin Pitt) with the Ute on the Flat the day we brought it back for restoration*

The tyres were shot, there was rust in just about every part. Surprisingly, even after breaking down, Dad would put petrol into the carburettor and it would start. This had stopped by 2013 with the motor seized.

It still had the original key… thank heavens!

At the point we picked it up, we still believed $15-$20K would bring her up to scratch. If only we'd been better prepared, because it cost a lot more than that.

We drove it up to Gayndah

and it sat at the mechanics until into 2015 ready to begin. Along the way there were some incidents and accidents that held us up until July 2015 when we began the restoration in earnest.

## Restoration of the WB

### HOW MANY OTHER WRECKS ARE NEEDED TO RESTORE ONE WB?

The first image shows the non-reconditioned chassis. Every part of the vehicle was disassembled.

The rims were removed, blasted, repainted and new tyres put on it. Then they went back on so the chassis could be moved around.

*Trivia: As I was the second owner, and never made modifications/changes to the wheels, these are still the original rims it rolled off the assembly line floor with.*

In the beginning we had vehicle disassembly commencing. The body and tray were pulled off. The nose cone was removed and the interior gutted ready to begin work.

The rust was everywhere, cancer eating her out almost to the point of no-return. Any longer on the hill, and she would have been beyond saving.

At this point every bolt, nut and wire were removed, cleaned and inspected so we could discover what was salvageable and what required replacement.

At this stage, we discovered the existence of other wrecks that could be used as donors to complete this long-running project.

The decision was made at this point as to how close to factory release we would make it. It was important to restore it to showroom floor condition, without modifications and as I remembered it back when I drove it.

The original 202 Blue (3.3L Holden Motor) a straight 6 hadn't been started in years (well, not since the old Carburettor story!) This was a Repco long motor after I blew up the original in Goodna. (Great days, those!) I nearly put the conrod through the side of the block and Mr Van Ansem (mechanic) stood there shaking his head. "Mark, what did you do? They nearly wouldn't trade the motor."

I was exceptionally pleased to find the original key was still in the ignition. At least we didn't need to replace the barrels and complications that would bring!

When I used to pull up at the service station, I would often joke, "check the petrol and fill up the oil." I'd buy the cheap thick oil because the engine used so much that the oil would plug it up and slow the oil loss.

*The reconditioned Chassis with an HZ 308 motor (not mine) using it for sizing with a 4 speed gear box. It has the new fuel tank, causing us no end of trouble.*

*The body/cabin restored.*

Major milestone in 2015, the body was glass bead blasted and repaired. This meant the body was ready for painting in the Palais White of its time.

It's weird to see the body naked like this.

*Painted in Palais White.*

This was the next stage of setting the tone of the restoration. Once we had the body painted, the quality of the restoration work was so high, that I couldn't bring myself to short cut the job. This was the time where the quality was set.

At this point, the gear box was stripped down. This is the stock standard column shift, '3 on the three' with reverse. After all the years of both use then sitting, it was as good as the day it was manufactured. All that was changed was the clutch bearing, because while we were in there, it was better to do this straight away, not that it probably *had* to be replaced. You can't kill an old holden with a stick!

*The gear box.*

*The body on the chassis.*

The body sat for a while (hmm two months) between the painting and moving onto the chassis part.

In December 2015, the engine and gearbox were joined then set in place on the chassis. At this time, the reassembly finally commenced!

It's a long journey back, that started but it would take years before we could drive it, yet.

In January 2017, it went back into the workshop and more components were added to the engine bay. The panel restoration work was started for the rest of the body.

The alternator and the exhaust manifolds are finally in place. Everything was done in bursts around other pieces Norm was working on, hence the long breaks in between images and work.

Whilst the mechanical work went on, every panel was fully restored. All the rust was removed (including cutting and prefabrication as required) to original specifications.

*The door sandblasted prior to painting and back to primer*

*Bonnet grill and bonnet*

Stan repaired and repainted every piece before it was meticulously reassembled so the end result was seamless.

Whole sections of the body work were eaten away with the rust, so fabrication was vitally important to ensuring that every part not only fit, but was perfect.

It had already been a long process and work occurred sporadically to align with other commitments.

By this stage, we had 3 donor vehicles as well as the original, I'd driven.

The fuel tank, as mentioned earlier, continued to prove problematic.

**Question:** *Do you know how hard it is to get a fuel sender unit that works correctly for a WB? We began to* suspect this was a GMH conspiracy to ensure the fuel gauge did not work accurately! One was salvaged from one of the three donor vehicles and we **thought** we had addressed the issue. It was one of the peculiarities of the rebuild that it was small parts that posed the greatest issues.

*The primed door and the body is almost complete - at least cosmetically.*

*The original seats were in poor repair and needed total replacement of the covers.*

The upholstery of the bench seat was in poor condition at the beginning of the reconstruction. It was necessary to send it away for specialist restoration. While the springs were in reasonable condition, a total recovering of the seat was necessary.

This took some considerable time but the end result was well worth the extra effort.

As with all other aspects, it was important to ensure the

colours were as original as possible. We have had to refer to Holden Commercial Services and Repairs Guide Book (Gregory's) along with judicious online searching and working with companies who specialise in the parts for restoration projects.

*With the upholstery back in town, it's almost ready to go in.*

The Radiator Support Panel had the base rusted out - which apparently is fairly common - so the base had to be refabricated after we chose the best of the donor spares.

The braking system was horrifically expensive and is a combination of 'new' and donor parts, but by October 2017 it was installed.

By November 2017 the front panels, nose cone, bonnet and the tail gate were finished and installed.

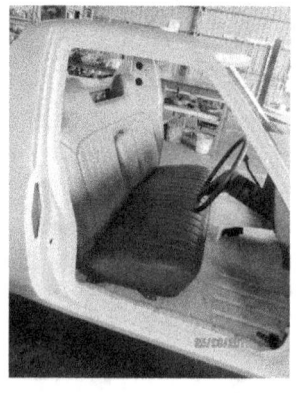

*Finally the new seat in installed*

The tail gate were rusted to the point of not being salvageable, and again this seems to be inherent in the vehicle. Even with 3 donor vehicles, there wasn't one in useable condition. Thankfully we were able to buy a total replacement, which sits perfectly.

## When the Phoenix Rises

*Radiator Support Nose Cone and Brake components are installed, including the Master Cylinder.*

By this stage, with the panel work mostly completed, Norm took to keeping the ute in his personal garage along with his own project car.

It was clear we wouldn't have it for Christmas 2017 but we were hopeful, as the vehicle was now getting close to finished, we'd have it in 2018, but alas, as you'll see that didn't quite come to pass.

At the end of 2017, we made note that the radiator support system and the electrical system had commenced reconstruction and the brake system was in place with brake fluid in the reservoirs.

And of course, our family newsletter was noting: *The Ute story for 2018 started with the immortal words "I have a quiet time over January and will get in and get this finished."*

*Lights are in, the grill is completed and just waiting on the bumper bar and final pieces.*

And then the bumper bar went on.

The body work was completed except for bits like the mirrors but they would come toward the end.

When we finished the body work, the motor was turned over for the first time since the rebuild. This was a pivotal moment and met with great fanfare.

That's when we discovered the ignition switch had seen better days. It was replaced at that time.

By the end of 2018 we noted in our annual newsletter (and the saga of the Ute): *the front bumper bar is on and a new windshield wiper reservoir and radiator overflow plus the horn works – bonus. All the rubber seals are in and the glass is in so the cabin is finally isolated from the elements. The rear tray brought back to the point of being ready to be spray painted. Whilst it doesn't seem much each one is a significant step towards the path of being roadworthy.*

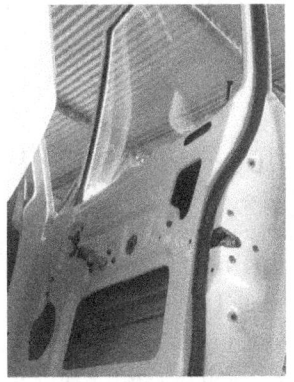

With the completion of the external body works, focus turned to the interior and while it's difficult to see, all the glass was placed back into the vehicle, making it weatherproof once again.

This was the beginning of the end for the interior.

The interior door trims were not salvageable due to the damage of sitting on the hill for many years, so it was necessary to track down new trims. These are custom cut to order.

You'll notice there are no cutouts for the window winder, as these are done at the time of installation.

We did manage to salvage the original door rests though and this was significant as with a little TLC they look pretty good and tell some of the story of the vehicle. There is also a metal strip at the top of the door trims. It's the thing that hooks in and holds the trims in place. Thankfully the piece we had was undamaged and able to be reused.

It's all the small bits that you don't necessarily think of when you first begin that caused issues all the way along.

While I originally had a Clarion International Sound

System back in the days when I drove the ute in Brisbane, I wanted to keep the vehicle as original as possible. I had initially considered reconditioning the one I had but in December 2019 I managed to track down an original GMH radio.

*GMH Radio*

It seems silly, but it allowed me to keep the original feel of the vehicle. The bonus was, it fit, without needing to cut anything out in the dash.

I purchased a modern radio and speakers (inset by the firewall) so I could actually listen to music and bluetooth my phone. This is one of the few modern things that we did, however, we had that mounted low under the dash and mostly out of sight.

The dash was pretty close to derelict when we pulled it off the hill.

Back when I drove the ute in Brisbane it was rare that

anything on the dash worked accurately. My wife would say, at all!

*The dash in 2017*

*The dash in 2019*

Remember that troublesome fuel sender unit? After 4 different sender units, one of which was purchased new from a spare parts specialist, it still doesn't work! It's nice to see some aspects of the original Holden remain exactly the same.

The dash wasn't altered or cut (as I explained earlier) so it's still in original condition and the GMH radio slid in, just like a knife in butter.

We complemented the vehicle with a spring mounted aerial which was of its time and keeps the original flavour. While I originally had a CB unit I have decided not to replace it.

*The completed dash*

The tail light lenses proved no issue, but apparently another flaw with the WB's has been in sourcing the tail light assembly unit (the bit the bulb goes into) and that held us up for some considerable time while we located what we needed. The rear bumperettes were easier to find.

The light surrounds were extremely difficult to find. They look like chrome but are in actual fact plastic. Because of the construction they haven't lasted and prove hard to find. As a result, people who do have them know their value. This was slightly ouch to purchase.

*Finally, with registration plates.*

In February 2020 the ute moved to the next major step. While the vehicle wasn't quite ready to register, the registration plates were put onto the car. This was really the home run started.

*The back tray is spray painted.*

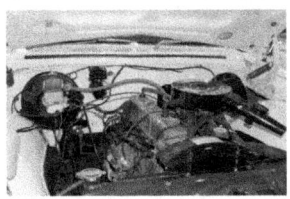

*The completed engine*

*The carburettor*

The final bodywork was completed with the respray of the back tray. The engine had finally been fired up for the first time in years on 5th October 2018 - this. Was the first time since she'd been parked on the hill, and for me I could finally see the reward for effort.

The carburettor is the original unit, as is the long motor I put in place (though it was fully rebuilt) with a new cam shaft. The wiring has been completely replaced and renewed. There is not a single original piece of wiring left in it.

The car now ran like a champion, however until the final week before pick up, there was an annoying miss and it would drop out to 5 cylinders. After extensive checks (down to tryng a replacement carburettor) the issue turned out to be the valve springs. Having overheated the motor once or twice (or many more times) the springs had softened to the point where they were no longer seated properly and required replacement. That means the vehicle probably hadn't run properly for many years and would possibly have contributed to the mechanical failure leading to it being parked on the hill. The carburettor, in the end, did not need replacing.

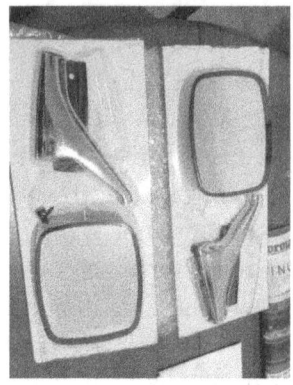

The left-hand side (passenger) mirrors that were on the car were missing, so while we could have purchased a single mirror, it made sense to renew them both at the point in preparation for registration. These were purchased new from a specialist stockist.

*Side Mirrors*

Now that the roadworthy had finally been completed, it was the day of registration. After many long years, it would be back on the road once more. 6th April, 2020 was a milestone in the story of the Ute.

**All that was left, was to arrange a date for pickup.
The excitement was building.**

## Finishing Touches

No vehicle is complete without the personalised plates. Ordered in 2015 - well ahead of need - we chose MJP for Mark Pitt and the 281 is indicative of its February build date in 1981. (Per the compliance date.)

Of course, we had the original key, but finding even a keychain suitable for the key proved difficult.

Being the only key in living existence, I've attempted to source a GM branded key blank but without any success. I'll keep trying to find the appropriate key blanks, but it's time to order spare keys just in case the original goes missing.

## Restored and Returned

*Finally picking up the Ute. Great props to Norm for his efforts over the last seven years during the reconstruction.*

On a cool and overcast May day, we headed to Gayndah to pick up the Ute. Of course, as is the usual, the heater didn't work. (Thankfully I was rugged up for the cool weather) but on the bright side, the handbrake has never worked so well!

*After 7 years it's finally back home where it belongs!*

As it rolled out of the garage for the first time, I can't express how much excitement was filling me. Surreal isn't the right word, but it was a long journey coming to the finalisation of this stage.

I will admit to a satisfaction knowing I'd saved a piece of Holden's and Australia's history in this one car.

On the journey home I rediscovered the weight of the vehicle and the realisation I hadn't driven it in 26 years. The newer vehicles spoil you, while these older cars require you to actually drive them. While this may sound strange, the concentration needed is very different to the modern cars.

Memories flooded back of a different time when life

When the Phoenix Rises

was much simpler. (I won't go into the B&S balls or events - those are stories for another time!)

I drove the Ute down to Kingaroy and it seemed appropriate to get a photo of the ute outside the Holden Dealership.

This image captured the Old and the New in one go. It's sad to see the end of an era but at least this one piece remains - living history.

There will always be minor work here or an adjustment there on the car as we continue to motor forward.

There is still a long way to go to finish restoring this beauty to her original specs.

Among the forward plans are to reinstate all its original badges.

## Acknowledgments

This project would not have been possible without. The love and support of my wife Nicola.

It also would not be completed without the stewardship of Norm Cook, Burnett River Machinery. Norm project managed and oversaw the entire rebuild and it was through his care and expertise that the project finished with the final product.

Other people I would particularly like to acknowledge are Stan Medhurst for the panel work and Millington's of Gayndah Smash Repair for the paint work on the body.

A big thank you to Lynelle and Tracey for their proofing of the final version.

# Notes

## Specifics of the WB

1. https://www.uniquecarsandparts.com.au/holden_WB_technical_specifications retrieved 25 June 2020

www.ingramcontent.com/pod-product-compliance
Lightning Source LLC
Chambersburg PA
CBHW071545080526
44588CB00011B/1799